T0128467

BASIC LEARNING FOR EVERYDAY LIFE BY GOD'S TRUTH

Daily Devotional

Apostle Ebony Underwood

authorHOUSE

AuthorHouse™
1663 Liberty Drive
Bloomington, IN 47403
www.authorhouse.com
Phone: 833-262-8899

Published by AuthorHouse 03/28/2023

ISBN: 979-8-8230-0458-9 (sc)
ISBN: 979-8-8230-0456-5 (hc)
ISBN: 979-8-8230-0457-2 (e)

Library of Congress Control Number: 2023905731

Print information available on the last page.

INTRODUCTION

Growing in the salvation of the Lord comes with many trials and tribulations. Often times some days are more challenging than others. When you begin to look at life challenges through the telescope of the word of God, you will begin to understand faith in God's word brings you through. The bible tells us according to **James 1:3-4** that the testing of your faith produces patience. But let patience have its perfect work, that you may be perfect and complete lacking nothing. The only way this can be done, you must have a continual fellowship with God on an everyday basis. Your faith will be tried, but in the process you will be developed. Basic Learning For Everyday Life By God's Truth is a daily devotional. This devotional is to teach the readers how to navigate through life difficulties and challenges. As you devote yourself for 21 days and take in all that God is sharing, you will find yourself growing in the midst of your trial. This devotional will help you with basic learning. The word basic means the essential facts or principles of a subject or skill. God wants us to learn His principles and put to practice the truth of His word so we can develop a skill on how to get through every trial and tribulation. I pray you enjoy this 21 day devotional and allow it to cause you to grow closer to God. AMEN

DEDICATION

I dedicate this book to my Lord and Savior Jesus Christ. He is the reason that all of this is possible. Through His wisdom, knowledge, and revelation He has allowed this 21 day devotional to manifest. Also to all born again believers. Those that are striving to live according to the word of God. I would like to give special thanks and appreciation to my rock, my best friend, and amazing husband Bishop-Elect Mark Underwood. To my wonderful and loving daughter Minister Lashonda Jackson. To my two beautiful granddaughters Desiree and Laila and my grandson on the way. To my church family (THE HUB) who loves me and supports my vision.

CONTENTS

DAY 1
GOD WILL TAKE FOOLISH THINGS TO SHAME THE WISE

—⊗⊗⊗—

1 Corinthians 1:27
But God has chosen the foolish things of the world to put to shame the wise, and God has chosen the weak things of the world to put to shame the things which are mighty.

When you look at this Bible verse, you may wonder how is this possible? God is not complicated. He is all wise and all knowing. He has chosen, selected, and purposed the foolish things of this world, those things that will have you speechless, to shame the wise, those that think they are smart apart from God. He will reveal their ignorance. Also, the Lord has selected for His purpose the weak things of the world to shame the things which are strong. The Lord loves to use frail, despised, and insignificant things, people and situations to show His sovereignty and how All-Powerful He is. This verse shows us that God knows what He is doing.

We look at Jesus' life and we see that He entered this world born of a virgin, in a humble manger. He had no sin but He nevertheless carried the sins of the world. Although He was refused by many,

He still went to the cross to die for our sins. It looked foolish for Jesus to do what He did, but God chooses the foolish things of the world to put to shame the wise. Now our sins can be forgiven, we have the right to the tree of life and can spend eternity with Him. 2 Corinthians 4:7 say, "But we have this treasure in earthen vessels, that the excellence of the power may be of God and not of us." Sometimes we may assume we must be strong and capable, just to realize we miss the point. It is God's power! We are the clay and He is the Potter. It is Him that is doing the work through us. It may seem foolish to you but He will take what seems foolish to show you His Mighty Power. Be encouraged.

DAY 2
IT'S ALL WORKING TOGETHER FOR YOUR GOOD

––––––––––⟨∞∞⟩––––––––––

Romans 8:28
And we know that all things work together
for good to those who love God, to those
who are called according to His purpose.

What a sobering Bible verse! Let's look at this verse and analyze its context. The writer of this verse, whose name is Apostle Paul, was in a place of understanding. What he understood was the process from suffering to Glory. There may have been some unpleasant and very painful struggles he faced along the way, but he realized through all of those things, each experience, he had to put his trust in Jesus. He knew that, what we go through in life, God promises to use everything for our benefit. In these different challenges, the Lord always provided a way of escape. So this verse wasn't written based on assumption but it is based on experience. The word that stood out in the Bible verse is "know." He said "and we know." The word "know" in the Greek is Ginosko. It implies a very vivid understanding, a relationship between what is Known and the Knower. Through our challenges in life, we must come to this particular place of knowing.

When you are born-again, Jesus gives us the strength and the endurance to know. Now that we are in the light, we recognize, acknowledge, identify, admit and concede. You begin to perceive or understand as fact or truth. You will apprehend clearly with certainty.

First, you have to know before you can get to "All things work together." All things includes everything that seems impossible to get through or get over. We have all gone through some things that may have drawn us closer to the Lord. Instead of complaining, we learn to rejoice. Instead of being frustrated, annoyed, tired and wanting to give up, we think about all He has done for us. We think about all the things He brought us through and how He never once failed us. So, you begin to develop the words "And I know."

You may be experiencing some things right now.

As you read day two of this devotional, remember my knowing has to continue to develop. As you increase in your knowing, you will move on to the next part of this verse. "And I know all things work together for good to those who love God, to those who are called according to His purpose." The Lord has a Divine purpose for what you are experiencing. Those that love God will trust Him through the process and wait patiently. Don't give up! It's all working together for your good. Keep the faith, develop your "know" and stay focused.

DAY 3
DON'T LET ANGER GET THE BEST OF YOU

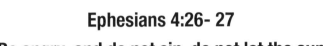

Ephesians 4:26- 27
Be angry, and do not sin, do not let the sun
go down on your wrath.

As we read this Bible verse, our flesh, our soul, the seat of your emotions, will, and intellect would not want to come into agreement with this verse. Anger is an emotion characterized by antagonism toward someone or something you feel has deliberately done you wrong. Anger is one of the basic human emotions, as elemental as happiness, sadness, anxiety or disgust. On Wikipedia, anger, also known as wrath or rage, is an intense emotional state involving a strong uncomfortable and non-cooperative response to a perceived provocation, hurt, or threat. The purpose in which I am defining this word for you is that the Lord allowed the writer of this particular Bible verse to be written for us, because anger is not a strange thing that you may feel sometimes. It's an emotion that God put in us, but He gave us the Holy Spirit so that emotion will be controlled. It's natural to get angry over certain things. That's your emotion responding to the situation, but the Bible says "be angry, and do not sin." We must understand that Jesus Christ died for the sins of the world and we now have the privilege to not sin. Our acceptance of Jesus, our belief in what He did, and receiving the gift of the Holy Spirit causes us to live a life that is no longer controlled by sin.

Anger is not sin! However, what we do when we get angry, can be a sin. When that emotion rises up, we that received the Holy Spirit can tell that emotion: "listen, you no longer have control over me." Whatever just happened and whatever someone did to you that was wrong, that caused you to be upset; you can ask the Holy Spirit for help, and the Spirit of the living God will help you calm down. Just because you got angry doesn't mean you sin into that emotion. God has empowered you to have the fruit of the Spirit, which is self-control.

The rest of that Bible verse says don't let the sun go

down on your wrath. Don't harbor unforgiveness! If someone hurts you, forgive them quickly because you do not want bitterness to take root in you. God is love and that's what He desires for us to walk in. I encourage you readers of Day 3 to let it go. Be angry and sin not.

DAY 4
LOVE THE LORD WITH ALL YOUR HEART, MIND AND SOUL

Matthew 22:37

Jesus replied, "You must love the Lord your God with all your heart, all your soul, and all your mind."

In this passage of scripture, Jesus is telling us that our love for God must be so deep and abiding and surpassing as an emotion or feeling. Let's look at how God defines love. The Hebrew word is ahab and it means to have affection for desire, delight in, or be fond of. It Implies an ardent inclination of the mind and a tenderness of affection, and denotes a strong emotional attachment for and a desire to be in the presence of the object of Love. The Greek word is agapao, to have a preference for, or to wish well, to regard the welfare of.

It is to take pleasure in; to prize it above other things; to be unwilling to abandon it or do without it; to welcome with desire; to long for. This love that Jesus is implying in the passage of scripture is a love that is beyond your human weakness. The love Jesus is asking of us is only done through our connection with Him; because He is love. When we think about Jesus' love we can hear the Bible verse John 3:16. "For God so loved the world He gave his only begotten Son, that whoever believes in Him will not perish but have everlasting life." Now that's love! His desire was for us not to perish and so He gave His life for us. He wanted to do it. He had a desire to do it.

He wanted us to have eternal life. This demonstration of love was beyond emotions. He prized it beyond other things. The agape love He has for us is unconditional and unfailing. When you accept Jesus into your heart, He gives you this love. This love must be developed inside of you so you will be able to do what Jesus commands in the Bible verse of Day 4. "You must love the Lord" is letting us know that it's not how you would love another human; our love must run deeper. It must surpass because what Jesus did, and does for us, no one in this world can do. This command seems to be impossible. Jesus is giving this command to those who are following Him. Those that are listening to His teaching and willing to accept the Holy Spirit. Otherwise it will be impossible to follow this command. When you accept Jesus, He fills you with His love. As you draw closer to Him, the more His love will be seen through your action, your speech, your conduct and your ways. When you begin to love God with all your heart, mind and soul you begin to obey Him in your way of living. Let's continue to strive and walk in what Jesus commands. We can do it because He did it. Amen.

DAY 5
COME TO JESUS AND HE WILL GIVE YOU REST

Matthew 11:28

Come to Me, all you who are weary and burdened, and I will give you rest.

Wow, what an invitation! Jesus is inviting us to come to Him. The actual Greek word is erchomai, which primarily means "to start, and set out." It usually has more the sense of set out because it usually refers to starting some motion. It doesn't mean start in the simple sense of beginning something, at least Christ doesn't use it that way. This is why it can be used to mean to come and to go. What the word erchomai does not imply is the concept of moving towards something, as our word, come, does. In Greek its meaning is different. The word also means to come into being, arise, come forth, show itself, find place or influence, be established, become known.

Jesus extended an invitation to start and to set out. Jesus wasn't asking us to start because He was the beginning of what He was inviting you to. It was now time for you to really experience something that was never experienced before. He didn't want us to move toward Him, He wanted us to be invited to live and dwell with Him. Come to Me is Powerful! Obviously we were in something that was not beneficial. According to John 10:10, "The thief comes to steal and kill and destroy. I came that they may have life and have it abundantly."

Before Jesus came we were under the control of Satan. This enemy is a thief. He will steal our treasure, kill our spirit and try to destroy our life. Then Jesus came to restore us, redeem, revive and reclaim us. He came so we can have life and live in abundance through the life He was giving. So Jesus offered us an invite to now live through the life He was offering.

It's hard work when you are working to try to save yourself or looking to someone human to save you. This gift that Jesus was offering was a free gift. You just had to receive it. It was offered to those that were tired of trying to live on their own. Trying to survive off of rituals and religion.

He said "Come," there was no force, but the invite was moving and influenced by His love. Jesus is always inviting us to a place of rest. This rest means peace, ease or refreshment. What Jesus is offering no one else can give. You can only get this through Him. Only He can give an intermission when life is still playing out. Let's go to the Messiah, the Author and Finisher of our faith. He loves you and He wants you to be a part of Him and He wants to be a part of you. Shalom.

DAY 6
HEAL ME, O LORD AND SAVE ME

Jeremiah 17:14

Heal me, O Lord and I shall be healed; Save me, and I shall be saved, For you are my praise.

Many of us go through tough times when we need God's healing. This Bible verse is about the Prophet that had a divine connection with the Lord and he was liberated to call on the Lord for help. We too, that have a relationship with the Lord, can call on the Lord and declare some things and believe Him for it. The Prophet Jeremiah said, "Heal me, O Lord and I shall be healed." Let's look at this statement of Declaration. He said Heal me. Healing means to make solid or whole. It means restoration of health, the making whole, or well whether physically, mentally or spiritually. He was crying out. Heal me is knowing that who I'm calling out to can actually do what I am asking.

The next words were important because he said "O Lord." Jeremiah knew the Lord as an Owner. The Lord was the Owner of him and he knew that only the Owner, the manufacturer that made his body is the only one that can Heal him. This concept is only through time spent with the One and only true and living God. Jeremiah understood that because the Lord was who He is. I have no doubt that this could be done. He said, Heal me, O Lord, and I shall be healed. In addition to its sense of obligation, "shall" can also convey high moral seriousness that derives in part from its extensive use. The word shall is used to express what is inevitable or seems likely to happen in the future.

Shall implies a promise, command or determination. We must understand that the word shall is a determined factor. When the Lord Heals us we are Healed.

The writer did not stop there. If you have been healed and saved before, you have confidence in the Owner that He can do it again. Jeremiah had confidence that if He healed and saved him before, He is the same God yesterday, today and forever. Save means deliverance from the power and penalty of sin; redemption. The only one who can deliver us, rescue us and redeem us is the Lord. He is the one that made us, created us and formed us, and He is the only one that can save us. You have to know who to call on.

The Bible tells us in Psalm 24:8, "Who is the King of Glory? The Lord, strong and mighty; the Lord invincible in battle." When you are in need of being healed and saved, you call on the one who is mighty and strong in battle, the one who is invincible. You can't lose with Him being your battle ax. He is the deliverer, He is our helper. We can call on Him and He will answer. He will heal you physically, mentally and spiritually; whatever ails you, He is able. Call on the Lord, He wants to help you, heal you and save you. Be like Jeremiah, declare what you shall be in Jesus' name. Amen.

DAY 7
TRUST THE LORD

———⬡———

Proverbs 3:5
Trust in the Lord with all your heart, And lean not on your own understanding.

Let's look intently at the verse above. The writer of the book of Proverbs' name is King Solomon. God had released wisdom to him so he can know, understand and apply this wisdom to his life. Not only to him, but also to those that read these writings. When we look at the very beginning of this verse it says, "Trust in the Lord." Trust in the Lord means more than believing in who He is and what he says; the word here for trust can also mean, "to have confidence in." Having confidence in something means having an assurance that leads to action. This was a command! Trust in the Lord was a command to let us know that the Lord can be trusted. He is trustworthy. The Lord will never fail. If we put our trust in Him, He will take care of us. The next statement is vital, because He commands us to do it with all our heart. Sometimes you can trust partially, because you are nervous about the outcome. We are commanded to trust with all of our heart. This signifies that in order to see results we have to trust in the Lord wholeheartedly without any doubt or unbelief. In the book of James 1:5, 6, 7 it says, "if any of you lack wisdom, let him ask God who gives to all liberally and without reproach, and it will be given to him. But let him ask in faith, with no doubting, for he who doubts is like a wave of the sea driven and tossed by wind."

For let not that man suppose that he will receive anything from the Lord. Wow, this is "powerful!" As you look at what James said, you can see that we have to trust in the Lord and not doubt. If we doubt, don't expect to receive anything from the Lord. We have to trust the Lord with all of our heart. This word "heart" is dealing with the mind. So many things can be in our mind to hinder us from trust in the Lord. As we continue to travel in our main Bible verse it says, "And lean not to your own understanding." This means do not trust yourself, because you are finite and you have limitations. Where in fact the Lord is infinite and has no limitations. You have certain limits and only can go but so far and can only do but so much. If we trust in the Lord, we cannot also depend upon our own ability to understand everything God is doing. In 1 Corinthians 13:12 it says, "For now we see in a mirror, dimly but then face to face. Now I know in part, but then I shall know just as I also am known." We only see part of what the Lord is doing. It's like seeing part of a picture that is not fully painted. If we are to trust Him, we have to let go of our pride, our ideology and our plans on how we think things should go. We can have a full plan based on what we think and it's totally opposite of what the Lord plans to do for us. So, people of God, let's trust in the Lord with all our heart and lean not on our own understanding. Glory be to the King!

DAY 8
YOUR HELP COMES FROM THE LORD

Psalm 121:1-2

I will lift up my eyes to the hills- from whence comes my help? My help comes from the Lord, who made Heaven and earth.

In this division of Psalm 121, verses 1,2, we can see the psalmist as being someone that has realized where his help came from. This is not automatically known. This is known through a relationship with the true and living God, who made heaven and the earth. The Psalmist starts off with, "I will lift my eyes." This is something that the individual has to determine in his mind. The word "will" means to express a strong intention or assertion about the future. It also means expressing inevitable events. This word "inevitably" struck me because it means certain to happen; unavoidable. So this was an individual that determined in his mind that I will, although it may seem as though I'm going out on a limb, but I am taking a chance.

This psalmist had a relationship with the Lord. He had to have tried this before, and got good results. It's so easy to have your eyes everywhere, but where they need to be. We have to be like the psalmist and determine in our mind, we are going to look at the one who made heaven and earth. The Creator and sustainer of the universe. Let's look at the word "help." The psalmist said, "I will lift my eyes to the hills from whence my help comes; my help comes from the Lord." The word "help" means to give assistance or support to someone, to provide someone with something that is useful or necessary in achieving an end. Wow, this is amazing! The Lord is ready to assist those that call on Him for His assistance. He's ready to support us and provide something useful or necessary in achieving an end.

The Lord has a wonderful plan for His children. He wants us to look to Him for help. He wants us to know that we are helpless without Him. We can't do anything without Him. According to John 15:5, the Lord says, "I am the vine, you are the branches, He who abides in

Me, and I in him, bears much fruit; for without Me you can do nothing." This is the truth! When you get in a relationship with the Lord, you will begin to realize that without Jesus you can't do anything.

The Psalmist too realized that my help comes from the Lord. The One who made heaven and earth. You would want to trust in the One that is the Creator of all things. The One that created you and me. He knows us and understands us. He knows how to rescue us and He knows when to rescue us. Just think about times when nothing else you depended on worked. You may have reached out to another human and they were not able to help you, but when you call on the Lord, when you lift your eyes up where He is and realize your help comes from the Lord, then you see results. He is our only help that can do any and all things. Place your eyes on the one that is trustworthy and He will help you. Amen.

DAY 9
BE STRONG IN THE LORD

Ephesians 6:10
Finally, my brethren, be strong in the Lord
and in the power of His might.

In this verse, Paul, the Apostle is writing to the church of Ephesus. Finally does not mean He is finished. It means He began the closing section of the letter, with practical instructions on how God wants His people to live. This word "finally" means at the final point or moment, in the end. Paul is speaking to the believers. It will be impossible for someone other than a believer to grasp this concept. The reason is because when we were not in Christ, we strived to do everything on our own. Having made many failures and causing a lot of hurt and pain, we realize as we have given our life to the Lord, our strength on our own is useless. Paul understood this concept, because he had tried to live on his own stress and it landed him on his face, needing the Lord.

In this verse Paul is encouraging God's people to be strong in the Lord. This word "strong" means having inherent power for being empowered. This power that is being explained is from the Lord. We must be strong in the Lord. We have limited strength. We can go but so far before we feel like we can't make it. This shows us that when we are in the Lord, His strength is made perfect in our weakness. Paul is striving to let the people of God know that you have to rely on the Lord. You and I have to be strong in the Lord. We must inherit the power that the Lord empowered us with.

Paul is releasing instructions for us, so when the time comes, we won't rely on our own strength to get us through the tough times, but we will be strong in the Lord and in the power of His might. God's strength is never depleted. He always has strength available for us. There were times in Paul's life when he felt like he could not take a situation or affliction any longer and he prayed three times for God to release him from the problem. After a while, the Lord's answer to him was, My grace is sufficient, My strength is made perfect in weakness. We, too, must realize in our own trials and tribulations that we have to rely on the Lord's strength and His power. We are rendered powerless without Him. We can't do it without Him. You can do all things through Christ who strengthens you. What a wonderful thing to know. The Lord knows you will be met with problems, situations and circumstances. He is here to give you the remedy to get through these things. Let go of your strength and depend on His strength, and you will see yourself able to make it through every trial and tribulation. Finally, my brother, be strong in the Lord and the power of His might. Amen.

DAY 10
PUT ON THE WHOLE ARMOR OF GOD

—⊰⊱—

Ephesians 6:11

Put on the whole armor of God, that you may be able to stand against the wiles of the devil.

As we dive into this Bible verse we must understand we are in a spiritual battle. The enemy's (devil) goal is our destruction. The enemy knows that we have victory through our Redeemer, Jesus Christ, but He still tries to wage war against us. We as believers in Jesus Christ must continue to use the weapons He has released to us knowing that these weapons are effective and they truly work. When we look at this verse and the revelation the Lord is going to convey to us, we will then understand why the Lord gave Paul this to write. Paul the Apostle, in a prison cell, writes this letter to encourage the believer what to wear during the spiritual battle. He was looking at the soldiers that were guarding his prison cell and the Lord began to reveal to him how to dress spiritually, although he was looking at the soldiers' armor naturally. He could see what the soldier had on was vital. These soldiers in the natural could not show up unprepared. The Lord began to download to Paul and show Him how we must put on the whole armor of God. This whole armor consists of having girded your waist with truth. This is your belt. It's like a pair of pants that needs a belt to hold them up. The truth is God's word. It holds us up when trials and tribulations come so that we can get the truth and it holds us together so we don't fall apart. It protects your abdomen and protects who we are in Christ. The truth of God's Word lifts you and encourages you.

You can't live without the truth so as a spiritual soldier, you have to have this belt of truth.

The next thing that's important that we must have is the breastplate of righteousness. In the natural, the soldier wears the breastplate to protect the arrows from getting to his heart. This breastplate in the spirit will deflect Satan's fiery arrows that come at us. As situations show up, we can repel. We can drive or force an attack or attacker back or away. We can repel temptations to sin or not live by our emotions. We need our breastplate on at all times.

We also need to have our feet shod with the preparation of the gospel of peace. The Roman soldiers wore battle sandals. They were thick with spiked souls, so that the soldier could anchor himself in the ground, and remain steadfast. No matter how the enemy tries to come at us, we must remain steadfast and planted in the knowledge of who we are in the Lord. Be anchored in the Word of God and your foot will be grounded like the natural soldiers.

Let's not forget about the shield of faith. The natural soldier always made sure they had their shield. This shield was vital. How they used it was important. These soldiers dipped their shields in water before they went out to battle to quench every fiery dart of the enemy. The shield of faith must be watered by the Word. Faith comes by hearing, hearing by the Word of God. Faith is vital to your armor. We must fight this spiritual battle in faith. We must believe we are victorious. We must know we are more than conquerors. Greater is He that is in me than he that is in the world. Keep the faith and don't go anywhere without it.

As we continue with our armor, let's not forget the helmet of salvation. This part of the armor is to protect our mind. When we put this on, we are putting on the mind of Christ. This gives us wisdom and grants us discernment. A mind that does not have the helmet of salvation is open to Satan's wicked schemes.

The last of the armor of the soldiers was what they carried, which was the sword.

Without this, the soldier was bound to lose the battle. Paul knew that this sword, which is the Word of God, was very important. The sword represented the Word of God. Without the Word of God, Satan is not going to back down. If we don't have the Word of God we will not be able to combat Satan's lies. In Hebrews 4:12, it says, "For the word of God is living and powerful, and sharper than any two-edged, sword, piercing even to the division of soul and spirit, and of joints and marrow, and is a discerner of the thoughts and intents of the heart."

Let's not forget to put on the full armor of God so we can be fully equipped for defeating the enemy. Amen.

DAY 11
IN EVERYTHING GIVE THANKS

---

1 Thessalonians 5:18
In everything give thanks; for this is the will
of God in Christ Jesus for you.

What a wonderful way to start this day with giving thanks. This Bible verse gives great joy because it helps us to see everything as a blessing and a lesson. It starts off with saying "in everything." When you look up the word "everything" in the Oxford dictionary it means: all things; all things of a group or class. It also means the current situation; life in general. Those that are born-again begin to understand that life comes with trials and tribulations. Sometimes these challenges make it difficult to say thank you to God when you are uncomfortable with the challenge you may be going through. When you begin to understand that every challenge you go through is testing of your faith, you must continue to give thanks. You begin to look at life's challenges differently. In the book of James, chapter 1 the second verse, it says, "Consider it nothing but joy, my brothers and sisters, whenever you fall into various trials." Apostle James had to have gone through some things to make this statement. He told us to consider it great joy when you fall into various trials. Get excited that what I'm going through has a divine purpose connected to it.

I know through experience that some challenges are harder than others, but we have to find a way to give the Lord thanks because that is the Word of God. In the amplified version, 1 Thessalonians 5:18, it says, "in every situation, no matter what the circumstances be thankful and continually give thanks to God. For this is the will of God for you in Christ Jesus." In this verse, Paul is speaking to this congregation to let them know to give thanks in every circumstance, and remember, Paul is writing this letter from a prison cell. He was going through some challenges, difficulties and situations, but he learned to give the Lord thanks. We must learn that in everything we go through, it's an opportunity for us to show the light of Christ. Paul was in prison, but the prison didn't have a grip on Paul. He learned how to praise God, and be content for whatever state he was found in.

We too, must find joy and rejoice with Thanksgiving. Having a thankful heart is very important. We are to be thankful and to continually give thanks. We need to express our gratitude to God and to the people He uses to help and bless us. Be thankful for the big and small things. When we begin to express thanks, we are reminded of how blessed we are. It is so easy to look at what we don't have and start complaining. We must learn to give thanks even when the flesh doesn't want to because we think the situation doesn't deserve a thanks. By God's supernatural strength, He will help us find a reason to still tell Him thank you.

Jesus is our greatest example of giving thanks. He showed us through His process while He was here on the earth to thank ABBA in everything. In the book of Luke 22:19, Jesus displays gratitude in the upper room. He took the bread, and when He had given thanks, He broke it and gave it to them, saying 'this is my body, which is given for you. Do this in remembrance of me.' This is amazing! Jesus at this point is about to give His life for us and He demonstrated thanks.

We know the Bible says Jesus is the bread of life. He

took the bread by demonstration, gave thanks, broke it, and gave it to the disciples. He showed us that even facing death you can give thanks. Hallelujah to the King!! If Jesus, our greatest example, can give thanks, then we too can give thanks. In everything give thanks. Amen!

DAY 12
THE JOY OF THE LORD IS YOUR STRENGTH

Nehemiah 8:10 NLT

And Nehemiah continued, "Go and celebrate with a feast of rich foods and sweet drinks, and share gifts of food with people who have nothing prepared. This is a sacred day before our Lord. Don't be dejected and sad, for the joy of the Lord is your strength."

When you look at this verse, you have to read the above verse. In verse 9 it says, "and Nehemiah, who was the governor, Ezra, the priest and scribe, and the Levites, who taught the people, said to all the people, this day is holy to the Lord your God, do not mourn nor weep." For all the people wept when they heard the words of the law. When it comes to the Word of God, it can be moving and touching. These people heard the Word of God, and began to understand what was being taught. To understand means discern, perceive, grasp, consider, regard; be perceptive, have insight. The people heard the Word of God and began to mourn and weep. The Word of God shows us as believers how to live God's way. This means making His priority our priorities, even when they are different from ours. Understanding and obeying scripture brings joy to our lives, and teaches us to acknowledge God. When you begin to learn the Word and understand it, it begins to bring joy to you. The 11th verse says, "So the Levites quieted all the people, saying, "Be still, for the day is holy; do not be grieved."

These people were encouraged by the Levites and Nehemiah. They were reminded that the joy of the Lord is your strength.

I encourage you who are reading this Bible verse to know, and understand that the joy of the Lord is your strength. When trouble comes, and you are faced with trials, remember to have joy. You may ask yourself a question, "How is God's joy our strength?" If you look at Hebrews 12:2, it says, "looking unto Jesus, the author and finisher of our faith, who for the joy that was set before him, endured the cross, despised the shame, and has sat down at the right hand of the throne of God." This is the answer to the question. Jesus Christ endured the cross for us. It brought the Lord delight to forgive us and save us. His happiness is showing love to all who believe in Him. Then His joy really will be our strength.

Nehemiah was encouraging the people through the Word that was read to them. Don't weep or mourn, or don't sorrow because the joy of the Lord is your strength. Have joy in the midst of sorrow and put on praise when things seem difficult and challenging.

The Lord is with us. His Word is in us, and the Holy Spirit is in us to guide us into all truth. So let's look at this Word, see what the Lord is saying and apply it to our life. Remember always, the joy of the Lord is your strength.

DAY 13
RIGHT AT THIS MOMENT, FAITH IS

---∞---

Hebrews 11:1
**Now Faith is the substance of things hoped
for, the evidence of things not seen.**

This Bible verse starts off with a powerful word; Now!
The word "now" means at this time or at this present
moment. We look at what the verse starts off with, "Now
faith is." Faith is not a complicated word. It simply means
belief and trust. This word faith is not a religious word
that is so difficult to do. It's a word that grows as you
continue to experience difficult things in life. As you read
this verse with understanding, it reads; At this moment
trust is the confidence of things expected even though I
do not see it. We must have faith. As believers in Jesus
Christ, faith in Jesus is what you need to regain your

relationship with God. Faith in Jesus causes us to see the things we have confidence in come to pass.

This author of Hebrews understood that faith is essential. As we begin to develop our relationship with the Lord, we will see how important it is to continue and stay in faith. Faith is not wishful thinking. It is an absolute conviction that God is not only willing but is able to accomplish all He promised to us, no matter how our circumstances may appear. When faith is present you can believe for the impossible. Many times I experienced miracles just by believing in God and standing firm on His promises. We must realize that the promises of God according to the scriptures are Yes and Amen! If God said He is going to do it, then believe He's going to do it.

Sometimes you might have to wait. You might even have to be put in some situations that will increase your faith.

You must know that it has a purpose, and the Lord, who is strong and mighty, will bring you out. I think about the three Hebrew men in the Bible. Their names were Shadrach, Meshach, and Abed-nego. These men refused to bow down to a golden image of the king at that time. Their refusal caused them to be thrown into the fiery furnace. What blessed me with these men was their faith. After knowing they will have to go into the furnace, they took a stand. And Daniel 3:17 said, "if that is the case, our God whom we serve is able to deliver us from the burning fiery furnace, and He will deliver us from your hand, O King." The 18th verse, "but if not, let it be known to you, O King, that we do not serve your gods, nor will we worship the gold image which you have set up." These three men took a stand. Although the odds were against them, they continued in faith. They believed that God would deliver them. They continued to say, if not, we know He is able.

We have to have that type of faith. The Hebrew men didn't allow the circumstances to dictate their faith. As you continue to read the story about these men, you will see they got thrown into the fire. It was three of them that got thrown in, but when the King looked in the fiery furnace, they saw a fourth person. The Lord was with them and the fire did not burn down. When they came out of the furnace, they did not smell like smoke. We must understand that our Lord is always with us. He promised He will never leave us, nor forsake us. We, too, will be in heated situations that seem like it will overtake us. This is when we have to use faith like the three Hebrew men. Remember, faith is not a complicated word. It means to believe and trust. We must continue to believe! Even when we can't see it, and it looks impossible, we have to trust that the Lord is with us, and He will help us. Hold on to your faith in the Lord.

Jesus told His disciples, including us that believe, I will be with you, always, even to the end of the world. Trust him! Amen.

DAY 14
BE QUICK TO LISTEN, SLOW TO SPEAK AND SLOW TO GET ANGRY

James 1 : 19

Understand this, my beloved brothers and sisters. Let everyone be quick to hear (be a careful, thoughtful listener), slow to speak (a speaker of carefully chosen words), and slow to anger (patient, reflective, forgiving)

Believers need to listen well, both to people and to God. It's vital for us to listen as stated in our verse for today. The amplified version of the Bible is telling us to be a careful, thoughtful listener. A lot of times this can be a challenging command. We often speak before we think it through. While something is being said to us, we are already responding before they can finish telling us what they want us to know. Sometimes we react in annoyance or anger only to discover that we had misunderstood the facts of the matter. The word "listen" in Hebrew is "shema," which means to really pay attention. If you are not really paying attention, you will speak out too fast and miss the facts of the matter. When you are listening, you attend closely with a view to hear. The author of this book understood as a believer, this is vital. We can make many mistakes by not being quick to listen.

We can hurt people by not being quick to listen. When you hear it all the way through you can then decide, because you have all the information.

This Bible verse goes on to say, "be slow to speak." Just because you *can* speak doesn't always mean you *should* speak. We must learn to guard our lips in what we say. In Psalm 141 : 3 it said, "Set a guard, O' Lord, over my mouth, keep watch at the door of my lips…" This Psalmist understood that they needed to keep their tongue from evil and their lips from deceitful speech. It's so easy to speak what's on your mind. We must evaluate what's on my mind, will it be beneficial if I say it? Just like the Psalmist and the writer James, we too know and understand, saying things out of our mouth too fast can bring death. The Bible says that life and death is in the power of the tongue.

So we must be careful to slow down before we say what comes to mind. Evaluate it and wait and see if it will be helpful or damaging.

The author finishes with being slow to get angry. When you hear this you may say this is challenging, because things can be said that will really make you upset. In Proverbs 15 : 1 it says, "A soft answer turns away wrath, but a harsh word stirs up anger…" This is the wisdom of God. It doesn't matter what is said to you, how you handle it will determine your victory. If you give a soft, gentle answer, you as an individual will experience the peace of God. You have a choice on what you will like to experience in the situation. If someone says something harsh to you and you say something harsh to them, it will stir up anger.

We need to understand that getting angry is not a sin. The Bible says be angry and sin not. We must have self-control. When something upsets us, we have to remember what the scriptures say and we will find ourselves living a victorious life. It's good to use the Word of God to help us in those challenging moments. Slow to be angry says we must be patient, reflective and forgiving. This takes the assistance of the Holy Spirit. You must be patient!

When something shows up, ask the Lord for strength to withstand and the patience to see it all the way through.

One thing that we don't do sometimes is reflect. Think about what's happening and how to respond properly. One thing we can be quick on is forgiveness. Let's be quick to forgive. Be ready to forgive whatever is being said to you or done to you. Your Heavenly Father sees it all and He will vindicate you. We must be patient and we will see that He will take care of the matter. These are some tools to use that are helpful as you journey in this life as a believer. Remember, be quick to listen, slow to speak and slow to wrath. Amen

DAY 15
BUT FOR ME AND MY FAMILY, WE WILL SERVE THE LORD

Joshua 24:15

"But if you refuse to serve the Lord, then choose today whom you will serve . Would you prefer the gods your ancestors served beyond the Euphrates? Or will it be the gods of the Amorites in whose land you now live? But as for me and my family, we will serve the Lord."

There comes a point where we all must decide if we are going to serve God, if we are going to put our faith in Jesus to save us from our sins and submit to His Lordship in our lives. We all have a choice to choose. The difference between choice and choose is, choose is the action of picking a thing or selecting a person when given a choice between more than one. On the other hand, choice is the work that has already been committed based on the decision and one of the available options has been selected. In this book of Joshua 24:15, Joshua made a statement of a choice that he chose. It was an affirmation of the family commitment to serve the Lord. God gave us a choice to choose. He is not a force! He would never force us to serve Him, but He wants us to decide to serve Him. God made a covenant with His people. He explained what He required, and the people said that they would do it. If you read Deuteronomy, you will see a whole generation did not make it to the Promised Land because they chose to not believe and serve the true and living God. In this chapter, Joshua is leading a whole new generation. He knows that they remember what was told about their ancestors and about those that were in the land that they now live in.

The ancestors began to serve a golden calf and where they lived, these people served all types of gods. Joshua had made a declaration to the people. It was time to make a choice. He decided, "As for me and my house, we will serve the Lord." As long as he lived, he would make sure no one in his family would worship idol gods.

The difference between Joshua and Jesus. Joshua

can help them outwardly, but only Jesus can help us inwardly. Joshua believed inwardly. Joshua believed in God. He knew that God was real. He planned to obey and follow God for the rest of his life. We understand as we read through the scriptures that the Lord expects us to make the right choice. In Deuteronomy 13:15, it says in the NLT, "now listen! Today I am giving you a choice between life and death, between prosperity and disaster." God put the option there, but as you continue to read, He gives you what you should choose. He doesn't make you choose, but He tells you the best option. As we are now in this dispensation of grace, God is yet extending a choice to choose. And in John 3:16, it says, "for God, so loved the world He gave his only begotten son, that whosoever believes in Him will not perish, but have everlasting life." This is the best choice you could ever make. Choosing to accept Jesus as Lord and Savior.

Choosing not to perish, but have everlasting life. As you read this 15th day, meditate on what it says. Make a declaration like Joshua did. In spite of his ancestors and people in the land, where he lived, he still chose to serve the Lord. Today in our society it's a lot of idol worshiping. So many things surround us to try to make us doubt, be in disbelief and unbelief. We must continue by God's grace to keep believing, standing on the promises of God and keeping our eyes focused forward. Make a choice and choose to serve the Lord. Amen.

DAY 16
STAND STILL AND SEE THE SALVATION OF THE LORD

Exodus 14:13 NLT

But Moses told the people, "Don't be afraid. Just stand still and watch the Lord rescue you today. The Egyptians you see today will never be seen again."

Throughout the scriptures we read the phrase, "Do not be afraid." The Lord is a mighty deliverer and He does not want His people to be gripped with fear. Afraid means to be impressed with fear or apprehension; fearful. This word "apprehension" means anxiety or fear that something bad or unpleasant will happen. Explaining the definition will help you better understand what took place in this Bible verse. The children of Israel (People of God that He chose) cried out to God. They were in Egypt and they were oppressed. They were in bondage. It was a form of slavery. These people began to cry out to God and He heard them and answered them. The Lord sent Moses to free them of this oppression and slavery. They finally were released. As they were traveling from Egypt, the king that was oppressing them decided that he would chase them and put them back in bondage. What I need you to understand is how fear can come upon you, but you must defeat fear.

These people were on their way to experience true freedom. While they were walking they realized the enemy was behind them. I need to pause right here and bring us current. This happened to them at that time but it happens to us now. When you have prayed and cried out to God for help or to rescue you out of a situation.

The Lord sends help and you come out just to find the enemy trying to oppress you again. It's almost like as soon as you come out of one trial, the other one is waiting to brew. However, God's words still stand. Just like He told Moses to tell the children of Israel don't be afraid, there is no reason for us to be afraid, if our God has already promised to deliver us.

Fear is natural, but it can be defeated. It is defeated by believing in what God says. Believing that our God loves us, and He will deliver us. We can be like these people. The Lord told them to not be afraid, stand still and see the salvation of the Lord. The word "still" means a situation or condition in which there's no movement or activity at all. In the Bible dictionary, this word means take your position; do not waiver in this matter. So God was letting them know to take your position! I already freed you so walk In your freedom. Don't give in because the enemy is on your trail. Keep going forward. Don't waiver in this matter. Stay in Faith.

When we are faced with challenges, it's so easy to give in. It takes spiritual muscles to believe God when the odds are against you. We must know that salvation means to be delivered from destruction. God had already promised what He would do. We people of God must hold on with a tight grip to what the Word of God says. These people had to no longer fear and choose to believe. We too must do the same thing if we want to experience the same results. These people had the enemy behind them, and the Red Sea in front of them. They were in an impossible situation, when it comes to man. My Bible lets me know in Matthew 19:26, "Jesus looked at them, and said, with man this is impossible, but with God all things are possible." I know I'm speaking to you who is reading this. Life gets challenging and we come across some things that will cause us to be afraid. We must know that God is the same God yesterday, today and forever. His Word still stands. Take day 16 and make it your reality.

Jesus loves you. He died for us so we can experience true freedom. The enemy will present things, but we must know whom the Son sets free is free indeed. Remember, do not be afraid, stand still, and see the salvation of the Lord. Shalom and Goshen.

DAY 17
BE STRONG AND OF GOOD COURAGE

---◦◦◦◦◦---

Joshua 1:9

Have I not commanded you? Be strong and of good courage; do not be afraid, nor be dismayed, for the Lord your God is with you wherever you go.

This is an amazing promise. God promised to be with us. In this particular verse, God was preparing Joshua for the Promised Land that He had promised the Israelites. He gave instructions to Joshua because He knew the challenges that Joshua would face. The Lord told Joshua to be strong and of good courage. Part of being strong and of good courage means trusting in the Lord as our true source of strength. In Joshua's case, he didn't have all the answers for the challenges before him but he was counseled by God to go forward anyway, acting in faith. The Lord wants us too, just like Joshua, to be strong and of good courage. In the book of Ephesians, verse 6:10, it says, "Finally my brethren, be strong in the Lord and in the power of His might." It's not God's desire for us to do this on our own. He has given us the Holy Spirit to help us. You may be experiencing some challenges and it looks like it's impossible to overcome. I encourage you to use this Bible verse and apply it to your situation, believe what it says. You will see things begin to turn. You will see your perspective change. You will begin to see things from a different point of view. The next set of instructions in this verse was for Joshua not to be afraid.

God told him that because He wanted us to know that no matter what we struggle with in life, He is always there, coming to us in love, and will see us safely to the shore of His peace. We have no reason to fear or be afraid. God made a promise and He will do exactly what He said He would do. We have to trust Him just like Joshua did. He did not know what was ahead of him, but God counseled him. He let him know, have I not commanded you. If He tells us something we can believe it because God is not a liar. He also told Joshua, not to be dismayed. This word "dismayed" means to cause to lose courage or resolution because of alarm or fear. We can't lose courage or resolution. When you have courage you are bold and confident. God wants us to be bold and have confidence. He wants us not to lose it.

When you look at the word "resolution" it means a firm decision to do or not to do something. Joshua made a firm decision to follow the instructions God gave to him. We too must make a firm decision and not let what we may see on the journey make us lose courage and our decision to go forward. The last thing God told Joshua was that He will be with Joshua wherever he goes. This was a promise. You can see how, as you read this chapter, God was with Joshua. God is also with us. Sometimes you may feel like you are lonely, but you are not alone. God promises to be with us wherever we go. No matter what life may present, you can count on God to be with you. He promised according to the Word of God that He will never leave us nor forsake us. Allow Joshua 1:9 to be your anchor today. Let this Bible verse be encouraging to you as you continue to navigate through life.

Don't forget the promises of God for they are Yes and Amen.

DAY 18
GO LOOK AGAIN

---

1 Kings 18 :43

And said to his servant, "Go up now, look toward the sea," So he went up and looked, and said, "There is nothing." And seven times he said, "Go again."

What we need to understand is we must hold on to what God said He will do. The Prophet in this chapter's name was Elijah. He would receive instructions from God and would always follow what God asked of him. At this particular time there was a drought in the land. It had not rained for three years, yet Elijah was absolutely certain that the Lord would honor His promise that it would rain. Elijah told the king at that time that he heard a sound of abundance of rain. So Elijah began to pray that the Lord would send the rain. As he was praying his servant went to the mountain seven times to see if the cloud appeared. This servant told him he did not see it. So he told his servant to go again. I want you to understand as you read day 18 that God is always faithful to his promises. If God said that He will do something you can rest for sure that it will happen. We must not grow impatient, and prayers we must continue to believe even when it looks impossible. During this time it was a drought. It hadn't rained in three years.

A drought is defined as a period of abnormally dry weather sufficiently prolonged for the lack of water to cause serious hydrologic imbalance in the affected area. That was the definition in nature. Someone that is reading this right now may feel spiritually dehydrated; when you are spiritually dehydrated you feel confused, lost and weary. Maybe you have lost hope and slipped into depression or anxiety. God must feel distant and quiet. Maybe you are battling spiritual warfare. However, God will hydrate you with His Living Water. The Word of God will always come out and revive, refresh, then build and restore.

One thing about the Bible verse that really blessed me was, Elijah had confidence in what God said and what he heard. He told his servant to go look again. Sometimes in life it is so easy to get impatient when we don't see what we need right away. It looks dark before you may see light. The Bible tells us to ask and keep asking, seek and keep on seeking, and knock and keep on knocking. We have to be persistent and we can't give up. On the seventh time the servant went up to the mountain it came to pass there was a small cloud the size of a man's hand, rising out of the sea. Hallelujah to the Most High God!! It happened just like God said it would.

Don't you know God will do the same for you if you really believe in His promises. In Luke 18:1, Jesus said, "We ought to always pray and not lose heart, your praying is not in vain." God will do what He said He would do. Sometimes you may get weary, but don't let it stop you. The Lord wants us that believe in Him to trust and believe.

If He said it, He will do it. If He speaks, He will make it good. Don't fret, stay in position, God will help you when you are in a drought. He will hydrate you with His living water so you won't be overtaken by the job. Hold on, help is on the way. Amen.

DAY 19
WAIT ON THE LORD

Isaiah 40:31

But those who wait on the Lord shall renew their strength; They shall mount up with wings like eagles, They shall run and not be weary, They shall walk and not faint.

There are so many encouraging words that are packed in this Bible verse. Let's look at those who wait on the Lord. This means more than just passing time. In Hebrew, this word carries with it a sense of hopeful expectation. It is a seed of faith. According to Hebrews 11:1, it says, "Now faith is the substance of things hoped for, the evidence of things not seen." The seed of faith takes your waiting into another realm. You are waiting, but you believe by faith that your waiting is not in vain.

In the process of waiting you are anticipating, watching for God to act. One of the definitions for "wait" in the Greek dictionary is push on. See, waiting doesn't mean I just sit still and do nothing. You push on as if what you are anticipating has already come to pass. In the natural when you are waiting for another human, they say, "I'm on my way." Sometimes they may have not even left the house yet to come get you. They may even show up late. The scripture is telling us, for those who wait on the Lord, it is something we can truly trust. The Lord is trustworthy, dependable, and reliable. Waiting on the Lord can be trusted. The most vigorous and powerful men may faint under strain and utterly fall, but they that wait on the Lord shall renew their strength. This is amazing because to renew your strength literally means to exchange your strength.

The word in a technical way can mean to exchange for something better. The Lord promises that if we wait on Him, He will exchange our strength in exchange for something better. His promises are packed inside of this Bible verse. He goes on to tell us, "They shall mount up with wings like eagles." The word "mount up" means to increase gradually in size and quantity. The synonym is build up. The Lord is telling us as you wait on Him,

He will increase you gradually and He will build you up supernaturally. In the scripture it says, "They shall mount up with wings like an eagle." When you look at an eagle and how they function, you will understand why the Lord allowed Isaiah to write this for us.

The eagle is a symbol of beauty, bravery, courage, honor, pride, determination, and grace. They weather storms. Eagles have strong vision, move with speed, and they fly high. The lessons we can learn from the eagle is you can rise above your problems, get out of your comfort zone, be courageous, embrace the pain. No one rules the eagle. They operate in power, freedom, and transcendence. Eagles have amazing eyesight and can detect prey up to two miles away. The figure of eagle wings was used in the Old Testament to represent the strength and loving-kindness of the Lord in delivering His people He had a covenant with.

As we continue with the verse there are two more promises. He said, "they shall run and not be weary, they shall walk and not faint." The word "weary" in this scripture means exhausted in strength, endurance, vigor, or freshness. The Lord is letting us know that this is not your portion, He will give strength, endurance, cause us to have physical strength and good health, also freshness.

When you look up the word "freshness" it means the quality of being pleasantly new or different. He will cause us to be not faded or impaired. This is good news, people of God!!

The last promise was they shall walk and not faint. First of all, we must make sure we are walking with God.

When we walk with Him, He gives us the ability that even when things are not easy, He makes things possible. Walking with Him gives us assurance of His presence and power in our lives. So, as we walk it will be impossible for you to faint. You will experience the power of God in you that will cause you to run and not get tired, walk, and not faint. When you feel like you can't make it, He will come to your rescue and let you know to remember what the scripture says. Hold fast to the Lord's promises, they are yes and Amen.

DAY 20
LOOK TO JESUS THE AUTHOR AND FINISHER OF YOUR FAITH

Hebrews 12:2

Looking unto Jesus, the Author and Finisher of our faith, who for the joy that was set before Him endured the cross, despising the shame, and has sat down at the right hand of the throne of God.

First and foremost, let's see what we are looking at. The writer of Hebrews is giving us a vivid description where we ought to be looking. When we are holding our eyes on Jesus, we are taking our eyes off our problems, situations, and circumstances. People of God, when you begin to observe the strength of Jesus and all the challenges He endured in His life on earth, your perspective changes.

We can use His example to help us get the better of or conquer our challenges we may face. The scripture lets us know Jesus is the Author and Finisher of our faith. He is the Prince, Captain, or Pioneer. Jesus is the first cause of our faith. Jesus came to the earth to show us what faith is. He blazed the trail of faith, meaning He took the lead. Jesus led the way, or He cleared a path toward progress. He made living this life possible. When you think about an Author, they are the originator or creator. Jesus is the founder. In the book of John, 1:3 it says, "All things were made by Him; and without Him was not anything made that was made."

Jesus is God in the flesh, He made everything including us. He knows our beginning to our end. The Bible says He knows the number of hairs on our head.

Jesus came here to bring us back in fellowship with God. He came here as the Son of God so He can be the ultimate sacrifice for our sins. The Bible says, "who for the joy that was set before Him endured the cross."

He wanted to come and give His life for us. It brought Him joy to get back in fellowship with us. We can look to Jesus because He can be trusted. The author of Hebrews 12 had confidence in the Savior. He knew that what Jesus did for us was not in vain. We have to trust and believe what the Lord inspired this writer of Hebrews to write. Jesus endured pain, rejection, betrayal, sorrow and so much more. In spite of all He had to go through, it brought Him joy. This was overcoming joy.

Jesus was determined to fulfill His purpose for which He came, which was to reinstate our relationship with Himself. All that Jesus sacrificed for us we should take no thought to look to Him. Don't allow your trials and tribulations to cause you to take your eyes off Jesus. We must remember what He endured and what it took to get back in fellowship with God. Let us lay aside every weight and sin that so easily besets us so we won't be so distracted that we can't look at the One who can help us. Be encouraged on this 20th day. Look to Jesus because He is the Author and Perfecter of your faith. Amen.

DAY 21
BE STILL AND KNOW THAT GOD IS GOD

---oœœo---

Psalm 46:10

Be still, and know that I am God; I will be exalted among the nations, I will be exalted in the earth.

Sometimes life can present some things that will make this Bible verse challenging. When life begins to happen, and unexpected things begin to show, it's so easy to get anxious and busy. It's so easy to direct our focus on the problem more than focusing on the One with all the solutions. This Psalm is teaching us to operate differently when life takes a turn or when trouble begins to erupt. The Bible verse is here to encourage believers to be still and silent before the Lord. This promotes a healthy rest in the presence of the Lord. The Hebrew word for "still" that's used in Psalm 46:10 is Raphah, and it means to sink, relax, sink down, let go, cease, striving or withdraw. The Lord wants us to surrender: Don't fight against His knowing. He knows, He sees, and He cares. He understands what we are going through and He has a remedy. We can relax in our trials. I know this is hard to comprehend with your natural mind. If you look to Jesus, you can let go and relax because He will give you rest for your soul. When we are faced with challenges of life this is when you will know that God is God. He is truly faithful to His word. We have to surrender our perspective to the way God sees a thing. The Lord wants us to cease our way and do it His way. He wants us to let go of our will and let His will be done in our life.

It's so easy to want to grab the wheel when someone else is driving and you feel they should have turned, or they should have stopped, or they are not driving like you would drive. That's how it is with the Lord. He is driving us, and we are to follow His lead. I know He can take some turns and take us to some places we never thought we would go. Allow some things to happen that you never thought could happen to you.

This is when you have to be still and know. At that time, you are fighting anxieties of fear and confusion. If we decide to rest and stop striving to figure things out on our own. As you meditate on this Bible verse, commit to the instructions. Always remember that being still doesn't mean don't move, don't do anything. It means you are willing to trust God and rest in His presence, knowing that He will show Himself to be strong in your situation.

As you have succeeded in your 21-day devotional take heart to all the things God revealed to you through His truth and let the truth transform your life. Be still and know God is God. Shalom and Amen.

ABOUT THE AUTHOR

Apostle Ebony Underwood is the founder and senior Pastor of Healing and Deliverance Temple of God in Christ Jesus. I'm also the founder and Dean of Potter's Will Bible Way Institute. I'm respected as an author, teacher, and preacher of the gospel of Jesus Christ.

As an Apostle, I am commissioned to build leaders and help them to discover who they are in the Kingdom of God. At this time in my life, I realize we are in control of our destiny. Everything I learn on this journey called life is my determining factor in how I will spend the rest of my life.

Basic Learning for Everyday life by God's truth will help you to understand the Basics. God is not complicated. He is willing to teach us through His Word. This 21-day devotional is to help build you up so you can have a more effective and promising future.

I have a husband who I love and adore named Pastor Mark Underwood, a beautiful daughter Minister Lashonda Jackson, a son-in-law-Terence Jackson, and two lovely grandchildren Desiree and Laila.

Printed in the United States
by Baker & Taylor Publisher Services